Cotton Candy Clouds
and
Chocolate Raindrops

poems about love and dreams

Felicia Carmelita Hardy

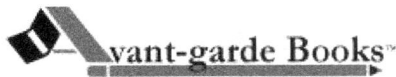

Avant-garde Books

Avant-garde Books, LLC
Poetry Division
Post Office Box 566
Mableton, Georgia 30126
www.avantgardebooks.net

Cotton Candy Clouds and Chocolate Raindrops
poems about love and dreams

ISBN: 978-0-9977566-5-4

Cover Graphics: Suzanne Horwitz

Dedication

To every human being I have ever loved.
To everything that I have shown love, thank you for the feeling.
Love shown and love experienced have always been my
inspiration and will be forever. Love solves all problems.

Table of Contents

Cotton Candy Clouds and Chocolate Raindrops
poems about love and dreams

*Song

The Cardinal

When I see a red bird, I wonder why,

it always appears when I am in cry.

It chirps to awaken a calm in me.

I believe it is God talking to me,

telling me there will be color in a sky of grey,

clearing the dark clouds of a gloomy day.

When I see a red bird, I think of my mama's words:

"This is a sign sent from the hands of God.

It is a gift for you that it will be okay...

that God will take your problems away."

When I see red bird, I now know why,

because God gave me this jewel to cease my tears of cry.

Us

To kiss or not to kiss,

there is no question.

Your lips are mine and mine are yours.

We taste love with our tongues and hold the world in our

cuffed hands.

When the dust settles and the moon shines,

we'll have each other.

Tomorrow and today are just capsules of progression measured.

Time is not important to us because it doesn't exist.

What we have is endless and relentless.

We've cut all ties with social constructs and what's the norm.

We grovel at passion and scorn selfishness.

Our ancestors hoped their lineage would find something like

this.

We understand that this is strange and arcane.

We understand that this is an especial union.

Indelible, classic,

us.

Our Power Together

I'm sorry my heart is powerful, but I'm not trying to overpower yours.

Look up at the stars with me and see the bigger picture.

Let's make our hearts design an earthly fixture.

Together, we can conquer the world.

I'm sorry my kisses are powerful, but I'm not trying to overpower you.

Come walk with me on this journey of troth.

Let our thoughts join and dance, seeking to find unadulterated romance.

Together, we can inspire.

I'm sorry my drive is powerful, but I'm not trying to overpower yours.

Let's celebrate life while basking in the good.

Let's make this union special like we should.

Together we can overcome.

I'm sorry my passion is powerful, but I'm not trying to overpower you.

Our Power Together

Let's be healthy in our search for happiness together.

Let's craft memories that will never weather.

Together, we can reach higher.

We can tread on noxious turf.

Lurking tragedies, we can curve.

Because we're together our vision is doubled.

If I see the ground and you see the sky, we won't fumble.

The bond fueled by our love makes us powerful.

It is When

Love is when the heat of the sun is cooled down by
the pull of the moon.
Love is when the rain helps the daisies grow.
Love is when a tree offers its branch to a singing bird.
Love is when the turtle can feed from the grass.
Love is when your eyes can recognize happiness with tears.
Love is when your mother tells you it is okay.
Love is when you walk towards a welcoming hug.
Love is when a child comes into this world.
Love is energy recycled from dirt to dust matter to atom.
Love created the evolution of life.
Without love, nothing will exist.
Without love, what is there to believe in?

A Destructive Encounter

The first man she knew was lonesome and cold.

How could he appreciate a woman lively and bold?

I don't know.

The meeting was of a twisted fate.

Bombastic sounds doomed of hate.

A love so bizarre and disturbed it was.

Mostly emotions consumed of fuzz.

Their encounter was not romantic...

dark, lust, manic

An end that was evident indeed, but not to cause panic.

She was the type looking for love.

He was the type looking for fun.

Love turned disgust,

Founding fun was a bust.

But this was later when the one big conversation

became a must.

Intentions were declared;

conclusions unwanted were bared.

It was never fair.

The ardor for touch was a fiery need.

They didn't want to just up and leave.

A Destructive Encounter

Bonds are never easily broken.

Those words should be more frequently spoken.

It is a sadistic trade to continue the path of disaster.

For this fleshly attraction, there could be seen no green pasture.

So, because they didn't want to depart,

their lives began to fall apart.

In time, their union comes to a screeching halt,

when they both argue that this was each other's fault.

When both realized their liaison was dangerous leading to no

remorse...

Their conclusion became this carnal abyss had taken its course

Describing You

Your skin absorbs the sun.
Your hair resembles that of sheep.

Your eyes are like rocks;
through them I can still see.

Your nose is a puzzle piece that fits next to mine.
When we kiss there plays music; God this must be a sign.

Your arms are like vines growing as they reach out to me.
The heat from your touch is 3000 degrees.

The sound of your voice makes my vision become blurred.
Your ears can hear the sounds of my body I thought were
unheard.

Your hands are like ointment healing my wounds.
Your chest is my safety; your heartbeat a calming tune.

Your legs are strong while they me hold up.
Your presence forever is still not enough.

Psalms 23

He lets me lie down in green pastures,

with no sudden disasters.

He walks with me along the ocean's silent waves;

he is my pilot that leads the way.

He is not God or Jesus,

just Adam shining light on the world's treason.

My soul is restored and his mirrors mine.

His righteousness leads me to where I want to be; it is divine.

He holds my hand in the dark with pleasure.

Before I was afraid,

now with his hand in mine and the tools he carries,

sinister territory doesn't seem so scary.

He prepared my tables with candles;

he doesn't welcome strangers.

He is not God or Jesus,

just Adam who makes up for past, terrible seasons.

Surely goodness and mercy shall follow me because he has my

heart.

I trust he guides it in the right direction all the rest our life.

I'll be in his house to dwell.

The lord is with us forever.

Psalm 23

He is not God or Jesus.

The lord brought us together.

Love is what we decided we will uphold.

We subsist through the psalms.

He is not God or Jesus…

I am the Eve that Adam went to sleep for.

.

"Not getting what you want can send you into the wrong hands.**"**

Confusing Two

I'd like to tell you I love you
but I'm not too sure I do.
I'm not too confident in my feelings,
I don't want to break my rules.
I've rejected love for so long,
I wouldn't see it if it bled.
I'm not too sure of my feelings
because my heart is crammed with lead

Okay, I love you really
I found comfort in concealing.
Wait...
I cannot say it.
I have no pleasure to display it.
Wait...
I'm too confident in my feelings and perhaps that is what scares
me.
If you would just be a darling and tell me,
about your love for me if you do.
I'm too sure of my feelings.
I've been fearful you may not love me like I do you.

*Chocolate

Peppermint candy cane swirls
but that's not what I want tonight
fruity juices dripping sweetness
but that's not I have in mind
because what I crave is much better…
better for me instead
bittersweet
tender milk
chocolate
Chocolate, I want you
Chocolate, can I have it?
Chocolate, I want you
Chocolate, can I get it?
Chocolate, I want you
dipped in a smooth covered film
savoring just for myself
teasing and delighting my taste buds
that's what I like about you
because what I crave is better…
better for any sweet tooth
I have a craving

Chocolate

much more degrading

chocolate

I want you

chocolate can I have you?

chocolate

I need you

I want you bitter but sweeter

Chocolate

The Elephant in the Room

We're standing in this room together and here lives something wonderful to give but hard to express.

The world has raised us to be patient for its day of reveal.

The world has raised us to believe there is a certain moment when it can be felt.

However, you and I both know you cannot predict its arrival.

It is nothing to wait for.

It is an energy force that commands you when it wants.

We cannot control it and neither can the world.

Together we stand in this room as it grows.

We're fearless in our thoughts but fearful in our expression.

Has the world turned us against it?

Has the world convinced us our timing is wrong?

That's the elephant in the room.

We move towards its force, but do not speak of its ways.

We feel its presence, but we do not act.

Yet, we're standing in this room as it grows.

We see it in each other's eyes.

 We hear it in each other's voices.

It pumps through our veins.

It settles in our minds.

The Elephant in the Room

We continue to not speak on it.

We're fearless in our thoughts but fearful in our expression.

That's the elephant in the room.

This is a majestic wild beast.

It is grand and powerful.

It is our reality and an energy that has expanded in such a small room.

We're fortunate it is here, because we know it endures forever

We're fearless in our thoughts but fearful in our expression.

That's the elephant in the room.

It was hard to address what was happening at first.

It's not a normalized concept to love so soon.

The world raised us that this is foolish.

It will be hard to explain to the spectators how.

Good thing they don't matter.

What counts is the dedication put in place.

No one tells you love births itself; you do not know the delivery date.

The truth is there's awareness here.

The Elephant in the Room

I love you, so soon, indeed.

We're fearless in our thoughts now fearless in our expression.

So now we're sitting in this room, proud of its growth.

Love, that is the elephant in the room.

Heart and Mind

Heart and mind meet at the neck.
I say this so you'll come correct.
If you're telling me that you can see my mind,
then I may be inclined...
inclined to show you I care.
So, enter at will if you dare.

Heart and mind meet at the neck.
I say this so your words can become erect.
If you're telling me that you mean no harm,
then sit at my table and put on your charm.
Charm is indeed something required.
I hope that who you are is what I've always desired.

Heart and mind meet at the neck.
I say this hoping my genuineness is something you can detect.
If you're telling me that you want me,
do better than tell and show me...
show me you have a spirit and soul,
one so unique, there's no compulsion to control.

Dreaming in Caramel

The ceiling is caving in and leaking something strange.

Something is seeping through the walls, something very

unordinary.

It's sticky to touch but sweet in smell.

There you are standing in the midst.

not uneasy…not affected

You're standing there pleasantly with your arms open wide.

The droplets are heavy.

You lift your head and open your mouth…

for the caramel dripping is just what you expected.

Your feet become weighed, because there's a creamy flood

taking place.

You don't mind.

You're standing there… happy… unwavering.

You welcome it.

Your head is lifted… your mouth is open…

for the caramel dripping is just what you expected.

With the caramel now at your waist,

you can get a handful of taste.

You know how to maneuver through the thick pool.

You're swimming in it.

Dreaming in Caramel

You float on top with your head lying back

You take deep breathes of the overwhelming aromas.

Drowning would be glorious to you.

The caramel wouldn't smother you.

You'd rather be here than anywhere else.

Dreaming in caramel is your choice.

Distance

Is it bad to crave your affection?

I just want us to make a real connection.

This is a confession:

please stop me from this babbling if you want.

These are not confessions I'm willing to flaunt.

Is it bad to miss someone that was never yours?

It's my lust for you that loudly roars.

I wish this was easy to avoid,

but to deny what's in both heart and mind is void.

See our distance is making this hard to bare;

it's not fair!

Please stop me if I'm going too far.

Maybe what's needed is for us to leave our hearts ajar.

Honestly my honesty is not even noticed.

I'm trying to keep it real and express my emotions...

to show you somehow, I've fallen for a man like you,

even when the distance only grew.

Conversations like we've known each other for decades,

stories and adventures we speak, cascade.

Without your presence,

Distance

life would feel mundane.

Our extant comfort cannot be explained.

Despite the distance interests are sustained.

I'm telling you I appreciate what you've brought to my life.

Finally, some peace and absence of strife!

Although the distance does cause anxiety within,

I must mitigate it for living that way would be a sin.

Remain my friend…if nothing more.

Your soul is what I adore;

you're what I crave for.

Distance may gripe us both,

but as long as we remain yoked, there is hope.

"You ever just wanted a kiss, any kiss. It didn't matter the

circumstance you were in, or who it can from. You just craved lips to touch yours so much, you would accept a kiss from anyone who was willing to give it to you.

Signed,

Basorexia"

My King, Your Queen

I struggled hard to figure out,
why before you, I lived in doubt.
A sheltered heart of stone and brick,
magician hands and magic tricks.
A master puppeteer for a lonesome dove,
you caressed my spirit with a satin glove,
bringing out my tasteful play.
Flattery consistent with no delay.
You made me forget my untimely quarrels.
You painted pictures for me of better worlds.

My King, Your Queen
you are those things

I care not anymore for male prey.
You have erased that desire and are here to stay.
You taught much to my tortured soul,
lessons worth far more than gold.
Now they say you only notice a full moon when you see it in
the sky,
and oh, my gosh is my head held high.
I am proud of what you have done for me.
I am happy with who I have come to be.
You are not deceiving, nor sent me coatless in the cold.
You have never harmed me, nor tried to consume my soul.

My King, Your Queen
you are those things

I could think of a million ways you have touched me,
regarding to how you delight to adore me.

My King, Your Queen

Your kisses relax my rigid bones.
Your gape upon me can produce intrinsic moans.
My ears melt from your tender words.
My legs jelly from your sinful moves.
You bare the build that a man should have.
You want to hold my hand on life's winding path.

My King, Your Queen
you are those things

God bless your soul, your spirit and mind,
I am quite certain our meeting is divine.
Maybe this will all end; maybe we will separate...
but damnit I will still trust in fate!
Indeed, I fear that day may surely come.
But to regret what I lost, I will not succumb.

My King, Your Queen
you are those things

This Season's Sky

I once painted a picture of a sky so blue,

to represent the endless possibilities with you.

Yet you traded me in for desert sands,

even after I put my life in your hands.

As an abandoned ship, I drifted at sea.

I stayed afloat but woe is me.

I weakened and decayed as storms pass,

but dry land I saw at last.

I crossed many lands to get to where I am.

My journey was long; I will not be the same.

As flowers bloom and trees re-root,

I'm given hope for my weathering gloom.

I realize seasons changing bring forth new creations,

and for me that means better inclinations.

Now that you're gone I'm a better soul.

Hardy I stand when the wind blows.

The grass is still green and the sun still shines,

even after you are not mine.

Lover Man

That man that does the work at night,

that man that holds you so tight.

He looks into your eyes and you know he cares,

that's the lover man: he'll always be there.

That man the tucks you in bed when he's about to go away.

That man that will continually make a way.

He rises like the sun.

He dreams of corrupting none,

that's the lover man: his legacy will live on.

His happiness shines.

He is consistently satisfied.

That man that creates possibilities.

That man that no matter what finds benefits.

 Rich or poor, vice or moral,

he will never choose a schedule over you.

Would not know where to find him;

I hope the world does not turn him.

Lover man be ceaseless in your goodness.

Wilt

Two lover gloves,
four distinct hands,
they were no model pair.

A love he planted all so well,
His was never a festering tale.

The ignorant mind of this ole girl,
She knew not a love so true.
She picked the petals one by one
until the flower no longer grew.

He tried to save its wilted roots,
before soon it would blow away.
Many times, she tried this too,
but love for her, would never take.

One day right before her eyes,
the plant was then uprooted.
It flourished well, quite very well,
a strange plot it seemed more suited.

This plant love tried to save,
yet it could not successfully do.
They chose peace in the end.
Maybe one day they'll meet in another garden again.

Dear Chocolate Man,

What I want to do to you when I see you is a sin. Undoubtedly, I've never been the type to completely indulge in my fleshly cravings, and God please forgive me for this growing lust. All I want, is to leech to your sweet dark skin; if I'm allowed. I don't ever want to take my hands off you.

When you're around me, you're like a drug. If ever it was possible to overdose, it would cause much more than the death of body. Somehow, I cannot get enough though. I've never seen an end to this obsession I have with your skin. Have you ever heard of Dracula? Well... I am it on you. All day, all night, you, and me.

Your arms around me send fiery, chills to my bones. I don't care where we go, as long as it is you that is there. I don't understand why you have my mind discombobulated, Mr. Chocolate Man. You haunt my dreams, stalk my mind... I can't wait until the next dine. I cherish your sweet skin. God forgive me for the lust I carry. It's a fact, I'm always anticipating the next time we meet: to kiss you, to hold you, to taste you. Chocolate Man, I miss you.

Love,

Me

Shipwrecked

All aboard for the lovers and wondering hearts,

the ones who have been internally torn apart.

The ship is due to sail very soon;

it departs from murky ocean at noon.

We all are here because we're trying to bridle romance.

We've been told there's magic at the scheduled first dance.

This trip is for those who seek relations,

those who want to anchor and divert temptation.

Finally, we set sea and hearts grow warm.

We wave goodbye to our past false alarms.

As the ship glides on waters true blue,

we mingle in hopes of futures anew.

Deceived at first are we at judgmental glances,

but we soon realize there is much forbearance.

We lessen our intensity and relinquish our guards,

just in time for the ship to wreck afar.

Now we deal with being stranded in nature,

but not to fear this has always been our mental state of

displeasure.

Shipwrecked

What better way to salvage ourselves;

with ebb there is the necessity to seek help.

So, all the lovers and wondering hearts…

all the ones who have been internally torn apart,

gather in hand to uncover the light of truth,

the facts that turned us aloof.

Just as we discovered the how's, when's, who's and where's,

the ship became fit for repair.

It seems that the wreck ensued a session of therapy,

the kind that's constructive and unique.

Self-love is now asserted at deck.

It all was by the guile of shipwreck.

Imagination

This is a propagation:

It doesn't take much concentration, to develop your

imagination.

a little innovation and cultivation…illumination.

However, the thing about imagination,

it can arouse grand temptation.

Creating sensation,

inevitably causing great frustration,

making you susceptible to persuasion,

of mass, unruly occasion.

Then there is the realization:

Yes! Needed is rehabilitation.

And after wise examination,

found will be the motivation, to refashion your imagination.

It will take dedication and organization…lots of affirmation.

Then, indeed will come emancipation.

Here is another propagation:

There is certain regulation, that comes with having an

imagination.

Use not for recreation,

Imagination

but only for inspiration and innovation,

or you will sink from its domination,

which will lead to mental consummation and mutilation.

Because then no longer is there room for revelation...

just a great deal of mental constipation.

So, there you have the elucidation,

from the complications of having an imagination.

"There is no better conclusion to any circumstance than to have embraced both misery and relief."

Tree of Mine

A possessor of great presence, you stand before me with
humility but you are so grand.
For every season, you pour nutrients and beauty into every life
source around you.
Your branches reach out to hug earth's atmosphere.
Your leaves tickle the clouds,
and your stumps tell a story

When you breathe in
you exhale world's most powerful vitamin.
But still you are elegant and meek,
not moving, at rest in the grounds.
Your love carries on forever because you bless many creatures
on earth

At daybreak, you shield our eyes.
At nightfall, you protect our homes.
In winter, you imprison harsh winds.
In autumn, you're a spectacular theatrical show displaying
dancing colors.

Tree of Mine

Pass the lives of our fathers,

you selflessly give and care for each generation.
You keep our secrets far beyond any sister or brother,
and prize history better than any textbook.
Between you and me, I hope they never take advantage of your

greatness.

Excuse me, do you mind love lusting?

Excuse me; do you mind me being here?

With every breath I take in your presence,

let it be known there is something enchanting in the air.

The letch in this room is intoxicating.

Please don't stop.

Love my body with yours.

Excuse me, do you mind kissing my lips until they turn pink?

Can you hold me until our body temperatures become one?

Come here and lay your head on my bosom.

Put your hands on my thighs.

Lick my body until it becomes raw.

Love my body with yours.

Excuse me, do you mind if I lock eyes with yours?

Peruse my skin.

Can I trust you to make me feel like the queen I am?

Come here and eat me up.

Scratch me.

Bite me.

Mark my body with your tongue.

Love my body with yours.

Excuse me, do you mind love lusting?

Excuse me, do you mind taking the time to embrace an

unwind? Give me spirit as our bodies dance.

Touch my soul.

Put my mind in a trance.

Don't make this an ordinary thing.

With abysmal energy, let our bodies sing

Excuse me…

Please…

love my body with yours.

Robert

I try to fight the desire that I have.

Tempted by your every touch,

but yet, I resist you much.

emmm, but I must.

Your kisses suppress my drive to leave.

You seducing me has been achieved.

Your hand grazes my body in a simple way.

It becomes a permanent decision that I must stay.

I lust now less so I touch you more,

I whisper in your ear "what are you waiting for?"

a taste of your neck and a stroke on your back...

an egg boiling to crack.

My legs are wrapped around yours; I'm holding on as you push in close,

for this what I am now ready for most.

Grounded

How is it that Pablo can describe the night skies so well?

How it is that Maya can eloquently describe a woman's quail?

How is it that I can't tell you right now what I want from you?

Like a tall tree, you stand,

Dark, brown bark you are.

Your branches are long and reaching.

Your startling presence is shade for any day.

They say trees don't move; but you always do for me.

They say trees don't talk; but you always have with me.

Your roots are engrained.

You penetrate me.

They walked on me and it hurt.

Except you made sure I did not shift or sink.

You feed me and I feed you.

We kiss from dawn till dusk.

We are grown through God.

You are tree… I am ground.

An Affair with Insomnia

I should be in a deep slumber.

Instead, my mind restlessly wonders

the greatest stories I've never unfolded,

while the haunting ones in my mind are boldest.

As they sleep, I'm tortured.

My brain is a memory hoarder.

To take curious paths is what I prefer,

since what is meant to be will be is what I incessantly learn.

My superpower is being a feeling denier.

Except when those things come rushing in,

I favor to engulf in my feelings of sin.

"Will I ever be great?"

This is what my thoughts intensely debate.

Will I ever fall in love?

In this thought my mind will indulge.

Yes, I have dreams deferred,

but not to be unheard.

Night walker and love stalker...

come all to observe the mental expiration of her.

This is what happens at two a.m.,

when the stars are bright, and the sky is dim.

41

Cotton Candy Clouds and Chocolate Raindrops

Cotton candy clouds, illuminated in the sky

They illuminate through my windows,

and I'm thinking…

I'm thinking about a moment so familiar so natural

yet so beautiful so wondrous

It was that moment I first laid eyes on you

The smile you expose from delight, I can see it

The lushness of your lips, I could taste them

The gray clouds turn sweet and cottony like candy

My thinking changes now too.

I'm reflecting

I'm reflecting in horror someone's lips on yours, I can feel it

someone else seeing what I see in you, I can sense it

chocolate raindrops

dancing as they fall

I'm thinking about a moment so unforeseen, so unusual

yet so beautiful, so wondrous…

it was the moment you reassured me I would be yours

the freshness of a new beginning, I could smell it the promise

of forever, I can hear it

Cotton Candy Clouds and Chocolate Raindrops

the chocolate raindrops teem bitter

my thinking changes now too

I'm reflecting…

I'm reflecting you taking back what you say, I can feel it

someone else enjoying your time, I can sense it

the chocolate rain falling from the sky

encourages tears to fall from my eyes

the cotton candy clouds gloomy now

encourages angst toward romantic prowl

and as the lightning flashes, as the thunder roars

I'm thinking…

I'm thinking…

this enchanted storm is hypnotizing me, causing a sweet

overdose in memories

as the chocolate rain pitter patters on the roof

I can picture your skin so smooth

as the cotton candy clouds sit high in the atmosphere

traces of your essence appear

hours of conversation are our source of cerebral lactation

Cotton Candy Clouds and Chocolate Raindrops

what is happening during this chocolate precipitation?
it is this enchanted storm that prompts the thoughts of you
but unlike the rain that I know is guaranteed to come unlike the
clouds that are sure to show
I don't know... wait…
I'm stunned at how quickly it had all begun and how quickly it
all can end
now I see the sun, and now I gain consciousness there was no
begin this is all just a dream, a vision it seems.

I don't even know your name or if we are one in the same.
how could these things be true?
I don't even know you
we never had a conversation

you never reassured me I'd be yours
there are no chocolate rain drops; there is no thunder that roars
no cotton candy clouds exist, none that may turn gray
I understand it
hope supports my reality

Cotton Candy Clouds and Chocolate Raindrops

hope that the possibility of our union will bring the two:

cotton candy clouds and chocolate rain drops;

a dream conceived by a future with you

Contact the Author

Email: feliciacarmelita@outlook.com

Mailing Address:
Felicia Carmelita Hardy
P.O. Box 566
Mableton, GA 30126

Business and book events: avantgardebooks@gmail.com

Cotton Candy Cloud and Chocolate Raindrops: poems about love and dreams is Hardy's debut writing project.

Available on **www.avantgardebooks.net**

THANK YOU for reading ***Cotton Candy Clouds and Chocolate Covered Raindrops: poems about love and dreams.*** If you enjoyed this book, please write a favorable review wherever possible. Also, feel free to share pictures of you with the book on the following Avant-garde Books' social media pages:

@avantgardebooks100

@Avant_GardeBks

@avantgardebooks

www.ingramcontent.com/pod-product-compliance
Lightning Source LLC
Chambersburg PA
CBHW060042050426
42448CB00012B/3105